SLIME

TIME

GET SET
FOR THE
SLIME
OF YOUR
LIFE!

make
believe
ideas

ANY TIME CAN BE

SLIME
✶ TIME! ✶

In this book, you'll find the easiest-ever slime recipes, **COOL CHALLENGES** in the Slime-Time Goo Games, **AWESOME ACTIVITIES**, and all the **SLIMY JOKES** you'll ever need.

CONTENTS

SLIME RULES

1 Always **ask an adult** for permission before making slime.

2 Always make your slime on a **hard, wipe-clean surface**. If you need to cover the surface, use a plastic sheet because newspaper will stick to your mixture.

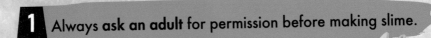

3 **Wear gloves** to protect sensitive skin and when adding paint to your slime mix.

4 When indoors, play with your slime on a **hard surface or a floor** that can be wiped clean easily.

5 Put old or failed slimes in bags and **throw them away**. Never wash slimes down the sink or flush them down the toilet because the goo might block the pipes.

6 Nobody wants glue on their clothes, so always **wear an apron** or **old shirt** over your clothes when you're making and playing with slime.

7 **Never eat your slime**—don't even try a tiny bit. Keep it out of reach of young children and animals who might mistake it for food, too.

8 **Wash your hands** before playing with slime (to keep the slime clean) and after playing with slime (to keep your hands clean).

SLIME-MAKING TOOLS

Head to your local **DOLLAR STORE** to put together your **OWN SLIME-MAKING** kit.

YOU WILL NEED:

Measuring cups

Measuring spoons

Small plastic tubs with lids—if possible, choose tubs with measures down the side as this makes it easy to portion out ingredients. Alternatively, old plastic food tubs with lids are great for making and storing slimes— just remember to wash and dry them first.

Large spoon for stirring (Use the handle end.)

Soda-bottle cap to measure out glitter and other add-ins.

SHINY SLIME

INGREDIENTS:

SLIME SIZE: 1 TENNIS BALL

- 1 cup white school glue (Use clear school glue if you want your slime to be see-through.)
- 1 teaspoon baking soda
- 1 tablespoon contact-lens solution
- 1 teaspoon washable liquid acrylic paint

1 **Pour the glue** into a small bowl and mix in the baking soda.

2 Pour the **contact-lens solution** into the mixture.

3

To make colored slime, add the acrylic paint (or any other washable paint) now. If you want, you can also add a bottle cap of beads, glitter, or another add-in. Mix well.

4

Keep stirring as the mixture slowly turns into slime.

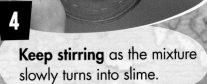

TOP TIP!

If you use half portions of each ingredient, your slime will set quicker.

5

The slime is ready when it comes away from the sides of the bowl without leaving any behind. Let the slime rest for two minutes before scooping it out. (If you take it out too soon, it will be a sticky mess.)

GLITTER WORKS BEST WITH CLEAR GLUE.

MUTANT SLIME

SLIME SIZE: 1 TENNIS BALL

INGREDIENTS:

- 1 cup cornstarch
- water
- 1 teaspoon acrylic paint and dishwashing gloves (optional)

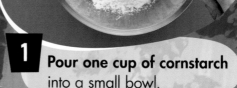

1 **Pour one cup of cornstarch** into a small bowl.

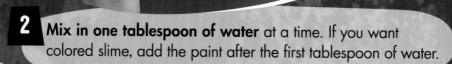

2 **Mix in one tablespoon of water** at a time. If you want colored slime, add the paint after the first tablespoon of water.

3 **Stop adding water** when a thick slime appears.

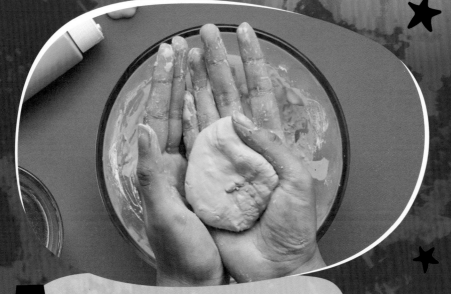

4 **Scoop the slime** into your hand and squish it together. Keep squishing and moving the slime around in your hands to keep it solid.

THAT'S WEIRD!

When you stop playing with this slime, it will get sloppy and watery, but when you squeeze it, it will become solid again.

9

SUPER-STRETCH SLIME

SLIME SIZE:
LARGE MARBLE

INGREDIENTS:

- 2 in × 2 in (5 cm × 5 cm) slab of white tack (tacky putty). You can use any color tack, but white is best if you want to add color.

- 2 teaspoons liquid shower soap

- ⅓ teaspoon acrylic paint and dishwashing gloves (optional)

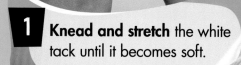

1 **Knead and stretch** the white tack until it becomes soft.

2

Pour the liquid soap into a saucer. If you want to make colored slime, mix the acrylic paint into the soap.

3 Dip the softened tack into the soap, and then fold in the soap and roll the tack in your hand.

4 Keep dipping and folding until the tack becomes super soft and stretchy like bubble gum.

SUPER-SOFT SLIME

SLIME SIZE: 1 TENNIS BALL

INGREDIENTS:

- 1 cup cornstarch
- 1 teaspoon acrylic paint and dishwashing gloves (optional)
- ½ cup liquid shower soap

1 **Pour the cornstarch** into a bowl.

2 **Mix in one teaspoon of soap** at a time. If you want colored slime, mix the paint into the soap now.

3 Keep mixing until a soft dough-like slime appears.

TOP TIP!

Try adding differently scented shower soaps to create beautiful smelling slimes.

4 Scoop out the slime and play with it in your hand until it becomes a soft, squishy ball.

AWESOME ADD-INS

EXPERIMENT with the add-ins that come with this book or try others of your own. Here are some suggested ingredients for making your slime **EXTRA IMPRESSIVE**.

SPOOKY, GLOOPY SLIME

fake bugs

peppercorns

googly eyes

GROSS!

LUMPY, BUMPY SLIME

 foam packing chips

 foam hole-punch dots

small buttons

TAKE NOTE!

Always ask for permission before adding anything new to your slime, and never add anything sharp or pointy.

SHINY, GLITTERY SLIME

 glitter

 mini gems and beads

table confetti

silver-foil hole-punch dots

TOP TIP!

You can change the texture of your slime by adding play sand or shaving foam to your mix. Add a little at a time until you like the way it feels.

SLIME STORAGE

Slimes last longer if you keep them in **TUBS** with **TIGHT LIDS**. You can decorate the tubs with **STICKERS**, **PICTURES**, or **FABRIC**.

Make a label to stick on the front or top of each tub. On the label, write:

- the **name** of the slime
- the **date** you made it
- the **ingredients** and **add-ins** used (so you can make it again).

Turquoise sparkly slime
18th September
clear glue, baking soda,
contact-lens solution,
turquoise paint, silver glitter

Secure the lid with a large rubber band.

RECORD YOUR SLIME EXPERIMENTS HERE.

Recipe	Result

TOP TIP!

Try twisting two small stretched-out pieces of slime together to create a candy-cane effect, and then roll it between your hands to give it a marbled look.

GOO GAMES

Get together with your friends to play the **GOO GAMES**. In this section, you'll find all sorts of games to challenge your slime-playing skills.

1 **The Goo Games** work best when one person acts as the **umpire** to set up the games and declare the **winner**.

2 The umpire should give the players **time to practice** before each challenge so they're clear about what to do.

3 Record the **results** on page 38, and cut out or copy the **certificates** on page 39 to reward the winners.

TOP TIP!

Glue-based slimes work best for games after they have been stored in their tubs for a couple of days. They will be less sticky and easier to play with then.

TOP TIP!

Use plain slimes for games because add-ins can weaken the slime.

SLIME TREASURE HUNT

PLAYERS:

any number

BEST PLAYED:

in the kitchen on a wipe-clean surface

YOU WILL NEED:

- 1 ball of shiny slime per player
- 5 coins per player

1 **Each player** takes five coins and a ball of slime.

2 **The umpire** then hides the coins in each slime so they can't be seen.

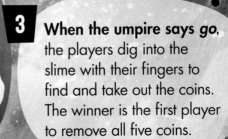

3 **When the umpire says *go*,** the players dig into the slime with their fingers to find and take out the coins. The winner is the first player to remove all five coins.

GAME 2

SLIME FALL

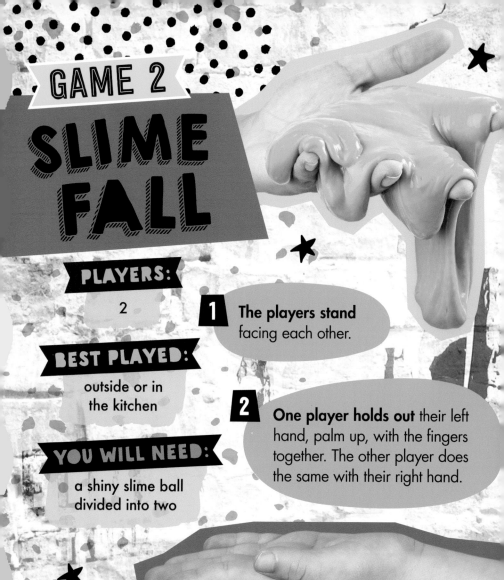

PLAYERS:

2

BEST PLAYED:

outside or in the kitchen

YOU WILL NEED:

a shiny slime ball divided into two

1 **The players stand** facing each other.

2 **One player holds out** their left hand, palm up, with the fingers together. The other player does the same with their right hand.

20

3 **The umpire places** half a ball of slime in each player's hand.

4 **Round 1:** when the umpire says *go*, the players spread out their fingers so the slime oozes through. If any slime breaks off, the player must scoop it up and start again. The player whose slime hits the floor first without snapping is the winner.

5 **Round 2:** this is the same as round 1, but this time the winner is the player whose slime hits the floor last.

SLIME FISHIN'

PLAYERS:

2 or more

BEST PLAYED:

on a kitchen table or other large wipe-clean surface

YOU WILL NEED:

- shiny slime (¼ of a ball per player)
- large mixing spoons
- four 2 in × 2 in (5 cm × 5 cm) squares of plain paper per player
- colored pencils

1 **Draw a fish** on one side of half of the squares. Use colored pencils so nothing shows on the other side.

2 **Turn the squares** fish-side down and mix them up with the blank squares.

3 **Each player is given** ¼ of a ball of slime.

4 **When the umpire says** *go*, each player puts their slime on the end of a spoon and turns it slightly, so it starts to drip, creating a "fishing line."

5 **Players catch as many fish** as they can by dropping the sticky line onto the squares and picking them up. Each time they pick up a square, they take it off their slime hook and keep it. If the slime line gets too droopy, players may loop it back onto the spoon.

6 **When all the squares** have been picked up, the players count how many fish they have caught. The winner is the player with the most fish.

GAME 4
SLIME STRETCH

PLAYERS:

4, 6, or 8

BEST PLAYED:

outside

YOU WILL NEED:

One super-stretch slime ball rolled into a fat sausage shape per pair of players

1 **Players pair up** and stand in two rows facing their partners.

2 **The umpire gives** each team a ball of slime.

SO STRETCHY!

3 **When the umpire says *go*,** the players walk slowly backward, stretching out their slime.

4 **The winning team** is the one that walks back the farthest before its slime snaps.

OOPS!

SLIME SEARCH

PLAYERS:

any number

BEST PLAYED:

in the kitchen on a
wipe-clean surface

YOU WILL NEED:

- 1 ball of shiny
  slime per player

- 1 blindfold
  per player

- 1 bowl per player

- 3 small slime-proof
  items per player
  (such as an eraser,
  a dice, and a button)

TAKE NOTE!

Do not use any sharp
or pointy objects.

1 **Before the game starts**, the umpire
puts a slime ball into each bowl and
hides the three objects in the slime.

2 **Each player is blindfolded,**
and then the umpire reforms the
slime in each tub into a ball.

3 **When the umpire says *go*,** the players use their hands to feel the objects and try to identify them.

4 **If a player thinks they know** what an object is, they call out its name and remove it from the slime. The first player to correctly name and remove all three objects wins.

27

GAME 6
SLIME RELAY

PLAYERS:

2 teams of at least three players

BEST PLAYED:

outside in a large yard or park

YOU WILL NEED:

- 1 ball of shiny slime per team
- 1 paper or plastic cup per player

1 **The umpire decides** on the course and the pass points where players will hand over the slime. Players take a cup each and stand at their pass points.

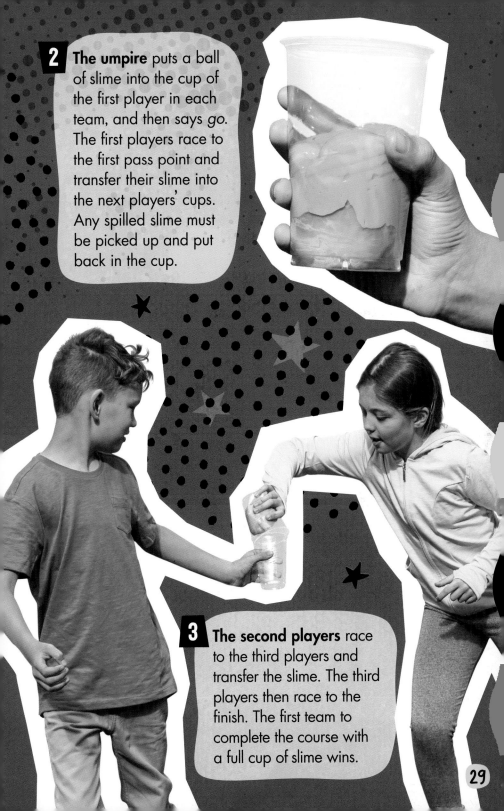

2 The umpire puts a ball of slime into the cup of the first player in each team, and then says *go*. The first players race to the first pass point and transfer their slime into the next players' cups. Any spilled slime must be picked up and put back in the cup.

3 The second players race to the third players and transfer the slime. The third players then race to the finish. The first team to complete the course with a full cup of slime wins.

29

SLIME LIMBO CHALLENGE

PLAYERS:

at least 3 (2 to hold the slime and 1 to limbo)

BEST PLAYED:

outside in a yard or park

YOU WILL NEED:

- 1 ball of shiny slime
- 4 paper or plastic cups
- a cap
- safety glasses or goggles

TOP TIP!

Use slime that has been left to set for at least one day—it will stretch better!

1 **Mark out two points** about 25 in (60 cm) apart using upturned plastic cups (A and B).

2 **Mark out a further two points** about 30 in (80 cm) apart (C and D).

C

A   B

D

3 **All players** should wear a cap and safety glasses or goggles to protect their hair and eyes from sticky slime. To start, two players stand at the points A and B and stretch the slime between them at shoulder height.

4 **Players take turns** to "limbo." Each player passes under the slime between C and D, counting the number of times they pass under the slime before it drops. Players can crouch, crawl, or limbo under the stretchy rope.

5 **When everyone has had a turn,** the player who has passed under the slime the most times is the winner.

GAME 8

WHAT'S THE SLIME?

PLAYERS:

2 or more teams of two

1 Use the chart on page 38, or draw your own, to record the winner of each round. Each team starts at 10 points.

BEST PLAYED:

on a table with a wipe-clean surface

2 Starting with round 1 from the lists on page 33, a player in each team chooses an object to make out of super-stretch slime.

YOU WILL NEED:

- 1 ball of super-stretch slime per team
- pen and paper for keeping score

ROUND 1	ROUND 2	ROUND 3
table	banana	car
chair	grapes	boat
bed	pear	truck
telephone	pineapple	mouse
cup	pumpkin	cat
bowl	apple	bird

3 **The second player** in the team has three attempts to guess the object. If they guess correctly, they get 1 point. If they guess incorrectly, they lose 1 point.

4 **Once all the teams have finished**, move on to round 2, and then round 3. At the end of round 3, the team with the highest score is the winner.

33

SLIME BUBBLE CHALLENGE

PLAYERS:

2 or more

BEST PLAYED:

on a table with a wipe-clean surface

YOU WILL NEED:

- per player: 1 ball of fresh watery slime made with ½ cup glue, ½ cup water, 1 teaspoon baking soda, 3 teaspoons contact-lens solution, and 1 teaspoon paint (optional)

- 1 reusable straw per player

- a kitchen timer or stopwatch

1 **Each player puts their slime** on a wipe-clean surface and rests their straw beside it.

2 **The umpire sets the timer** for 1 minute and says *go*. The players then pick up their straws and begin blowing bubbles.

3 **The winner** is the player to make the biggest bubble before the time is up. The umpire must keep a close watch on the bubbles and make a note of the biggest.

HOW TO MAKE A MEGA BUBBLE!

Stretch out your slime, and then flip it over quickly to create a big bubble. To make it even bigger, blow into the bubble with a straw.

GAME 10
SLIME TOSS

PLAYERS:

2 or more

BEST PLAYED:

outside

YOU WILL NEED:

- 3 balls of shiny slime per player
- 3 large plastic tubs
- pen and paper for keeping score and to label the tubs

1 Label the three tubs 1, 2, and 3.

2 Line the tubs behind one another with 3 at the back.

GOOD THROW!

3 Step back 4 or 5 paces from the tubs and mark a throw point line. It should be far enough away for it to be tricky, but not impossible, to throw the slime into the tubs.

4 **Players take turns** throwing the slime balls into the tubs and winning the points written on the sides of the tubs. After everyone has had three turns, the player with the highest score is the winner.

1

2

3

	ROUND 1 WHO WON?	ROUND 2 WHO WON?	ROUND 3 WHO WON?
GAME 1 **SLIME** TREASURE HUNT			
GAME 2 **SLIME FALL**			
GAME 3 **SLIME** FISHIN'			
GAME 4 **SLIME** STRETCH			
GAME 5 **SLIME** SEARCH			
GAME 6 **SLIME** RELAY			
GAME 7 **SLIME** LIMBO CHALLENGE			
GAME 8 WHAT'S THE **SLIME?**			
GAME 9 **SLIME** BUBBLE CHALLENGE			
GAME 10 **SLIME** TOSS			

Cut out these **mini certificates** to award to the **winners** of your games.

SLIME TIME

GAME NUMBER: . . . .

WINNER: . . . .

SLIME TIME

GAME NUMBER: . . . .

WINNER: . . . .

SLIME TIME

GAME NUMBER: . . . .

WINNER: . . . .

SLIME TIME

GAME NUMBER: . . . .

WINNER: . . . .

SLIME TIME

GAME NUMBER: . . . .

WINNER: . . . .

SLIME TIME

GAME NUMBER: . . . .

WINNER: . . . .

SLIME TIME

GAME NUMBER: . . . .

WINNER: . . . .

SLIME TIME

GAME NUMBER: . . . .

WINNER: . . . .

SLIME TIME

GAME NUMBER: . . . .

WINNER: . . . .

SLIME TIME

GAME NUMBER: . . . .

WINNER: . . . .

SLIME TIME

GAME NUMBER: . . . .

WINNER: . . . .

SLIME TIME

GAME NUMBER: . . . .

WINNER: . . . .

SLIME JOKES

What's a slime fan's favorite cartoon?

Scooby **Goo!**

What's a slime maker's favorite fruit?

Goo-seberries!

Why did the slime cross the road?

To get to the other **slime!**

What's a slime's favorite game?

Slime-on Says!

What do you do with blue slime?

Cheer it up!

What monster is green and sticky?

Franken**slime!**

How do slimes fix their hair for parties?

In fancy hair-**goos!**

What did the slug say when the snail played a prank on it?

I'll get you next **slime!**

Why do slimes always eat their vegetables?

Because they're full of **goo**-dness!

SLIME
ACTIVITIES

SLIME DESIGN

Transform these slime splats into **goo**-some slime monsters and **splat**-tastic superheroes. Then give each one a name.

Slimezilla

RACE TO SLIME MOUNTAIN

YOU WILL NEED:

- 1 dice
- 1 differently colored button per player

HOW TO PLAY:

Place your button counters on the start splat. Then take turns rolling the dice and moving your counters along the path. The winner is the first player to reach Slime Mountain.

SLIME MOUNTAIN

FINISH

START

24

8
GET STUCK IN A SLIME SWAMP.
GO BACK 2!

7

6

5

1
HIDE FROM A SLIME MONSTER.
MISS A TURN!

2

3

4
FOLLOW A SLIME SPIDER WHO KNOWS THE WAY.
MOVE AHEAD 3!

44

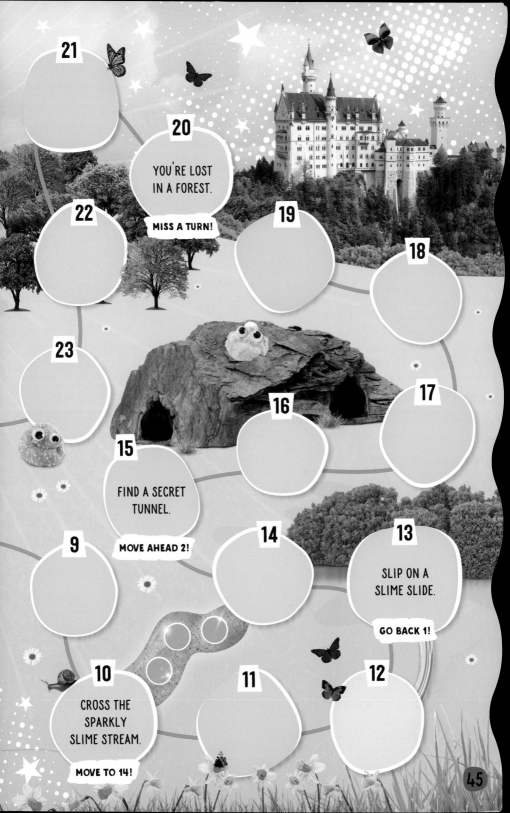

21

20
YOU'RE LOST IN A FOREST.
MISS A TURN!

22

19

18

23

17

16

15
FIND A SECRET TUNNEL.
MOVE AHEAD 2!

9

14

13
SLIP ON A SLIME SLIDE.
GO BACK 1!

10
CROSS THE SPARKLY SLIME STREAM.
MOVE TO 14!

11

12

Find the words in the word search. Words can go down or across.

Answers are on page 48.

GOO GLOOPY FLUFFY

SHINY SPLAT BUBBLE STRETCHY SLIME

MUTANT SQUISHY SCIENCE GROSS

S	L	I	F	L	U	F	F	Y	V	A	R	E	E	G	O
Z	H	B	B	A	N	G	A	S	Q	U	I	Y	Y	O	S
O	N	S	L	I	H	R	A	R	A	G	M	I	A	W	C
U	M	M	U	T	A	N	T	U	C	L	H	L	Y	E	I
A	I	E	R	W	O	E	C	T	G	O	P	W	H	E	E
T	S	T	R	F	B	U	O	V	A	O	T	A	A	S	N
H	S	O	E	S	R	L	L	I	M	P	M	E	S	E	C
G	Q	Q	R	T	S	S	H	I	N	Y	I	P	M	S	E
B	U	B	B	L	E	P	K	E	S	O	I	A	T	H	Q
U	I	M	M	I	S	L	Z	H	Y	N	S	F	L	I	U
F	S	F	F	L	R	A	U	U	L	K	C	S	D	K	O
S	H	T	L	U	O	B	S	B	N	N	I	T	K	J	I
P	Y	G	U	H	A	V	T	I	J	S	A	R	G	O	O
L	H	I	F	C	F	G	R	S	U	U	E	E	R	Q	W
O	T	E	O	G	R	O	E	P	D	T	C	C	O	U	R
O	I	A	D	T	H	I	T	L	E	N	F	D	S	I	A
M	N	E	I	N	O	U	C	A	C	J	H	F	S	F	O
G	H	R	E	C	L	I	H	T	F	E	A	E	N	L	A
X	S	L	I	M	E	N	Y	R	F	P	U	T	Z	E	Y

SLIME CHALLENGES

1 Find 5 slime splats hidden in this picture.

Answers are on page 48.

2 Play I Spy with yourself. Look around you and name one thing beginning with each of these letters:

S _____

L _____

I _____

M _____

E _____

SPLAT!

Find your way through the maze from A to B. If you run into a slime splat, you must start again.

A

B

ANSWERS

SLIME CHALLENGE 1

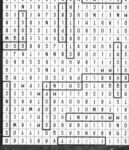

SLIME WORDS